EARTH
UNDER
ATTACK!

HURRICANE HITS THE COAST

Louise and Richard Spilsbury

Gareth Stevens
PUBLISHING

Please visit our website, **www.garethstevens.com**.
For a free color catalog of all our high-quality books,
call toll free 1-800-542-2595 of fax 1-877-542-2596.

Cataloging-in-Publication Data
Names: Spilsbury, Louise. | Spilsbury, Richard.
Title: Hurricane hits the coast / Louise and Richard Spilsbury.
Description: New York : Gareth Stevens Publishing, 2018. | Series: Earth under attack! |
    Includes index.
Identifiers: ISBN 9781538213070 (pbk.) | ISBN 9781538213094 (library bound) |
    ISBN 9781538213087 (6 pack)
Subjects: LCSH: Hurricanes--Juvenile literature. | Natural disasters--Juvenile literature.
Classification: LCC QC944.2 S67 2018 | DDC 551.55'2--dc23

First Edition

Published in 2018 by
Gareth Stevens Publishing
111 East 14th Street, Suite 349
New York, NY 10003

Copyright © 2018 Gareth Stevens Publishing

Produced for Gareth Stevens by Calcium
Editors: Sarah Eason and Jennifer Sanderson
Designers: Jeni Child and Simon Borrough
Picture researcher: Rachel Blount

Picture credits: Cover: Shutterstock: Tad Denson bottom left, Zita surround, Zstock center; Inside: Shutterstock: Tomas del Amo 9, Andrey Armyagov 40, Tad Denson 43, EHStockphoto 41, Paco Espinoza 13, FashionStock.com 21, Glenda 7, Iakov Kalinin 8, A Katz 31, Lakeview Images 32, Timothy Medrano 23, Nayuki 15, Paintings 22, Enrique Alaez Perez 5, Chris Warham 27, Leonard Zhukovsky 6; Wikimedia Commons: Jocelyn Augustino/FEMA 44, Andrea Booher/FEMA photo 35, Ann Froschauer/USFWS 33, LCpl Anne Henry 28–29t, Infrogmation 37, Mr. Larry W. Kachelhofer 34, Robert Kaufmann/FEMA 24b, Laslovarga 18, NASA 11, 12, NASA/Nilfanion 14, Presidencia de la República Mexicana 19, Eoghan Rice - Trócaire/Caritas 26, Jeff Schmaltz, MODIS Land Rapid Response Team at NASA GSFC 17, Jennifer Smits/FEMA 42, Mike Trenchard, Earth Sciences & Image Analysis Laboratory, Johnson Space Center 10, US Air Force, Staff Sgt. Mike Meares 39, US Air Force photo by Master Sgt. Mark C. Olsen 16, United States Air Force/Tech. Sgt. James Pritchett 38, US Navy photo by Journalist 1st Class Trice Denny 45, US Navy photo by Photographer's Mate 1st Class Michael Pendergrass. 24–25t, Russell Watkins/ Department for International Development 30.

Printed in China
CPSIA compliance information: Batch #CW18GS:
For further information contact Gareth Stevens, New York, New York at 1-800-542-2595.

CONTENTS

CHAPTER 1

THE MOST VIOLENT STORMS ON EARTH

Hurricanes are the strongest and most dangerous storms on Earth. These large, swirling, and fast-moving winds start over warm ocean waters, far from land. Some slow down and die out before they are anywhere near a coastline. Others travel quickly across the sea, crashing onto shores where people live. When a large hurricane hits a coast, the results can be disastrous.

Deadly Storms

Hurricane winds can travel quicker than the fastest train on Earth. These speeding, violent winds can flatten everything in their path and wreak terrible destruction. Deadly hurricane storms also bring sudden torrential rains from the skies.

The heavy rain can submerge land beneath large amounts of water in a short time, causing **floods**. Some hurricanes last for a only few hours, while others last for days or even weeks. They can impact, injure, and kill thousands of people.

Hurricane winds can whip up high, menacing waves as they blow across the ocean's surface.

Name That Hurricane

Hurricanes are given names because there may be more than one happening at the same time. Having different names makes it easier to keep track of the different storms, so that everyone can immediately recognize which storm is being talked about. Each year, the names are given out in alphabetical order as they occur, although there are few names beginning with the letters Q, U, X, Y, and Z, so these letters are not used. Some names are used more than once, but the worst hurricanes have their names "retired," so they are never used again. For example, Katrina, the name of the 2005 hurricane, will not be used again. It was one of the costliest natural disasters and one of the five deadliest hurricanes in the history of the United States.

EARTH UNDER ATTACK!

The word *hurricane* comes from "Hurican," the Carib god of evil. People in the Caribbean gave these giant storms this name because of their destructive power.

Hurricane Mayhem

This is what a hurricane strike zone can look like. Hurricane Sandy caused this destruction in New Jersey in 2012.

A hurricane's high winds are incredibly destructive. They can also spawn tornadoes, which wreak further havoc. Spiraling, speeding winds can uproot trees, knock over buildings, fling deadly debris around, sink or ground boats, and toss vehicles about as if they were nothing but toys. However, these deadly winds are not the only dangers.

Hurricane Horrors

When the heavy rains that hurricanes drop cause floods, water suddenly covers areas of land that are usually dry, drowning people and washing away anything that is not fixed to the ground. Heavy rains can also soak mud-covered hillsides, making the dirt so heavy and loose that it slides downhill suddenly. **Landslides** like this can bury anything in their way and can occur many miles inland. When hurricanes cause high waves that hit the coast, homes and businesses along the shore can be devastated. Anyone inside the buildings can be killed. In fact, flooding kills more people than the strong winds do.

Hurricane Scale

There are five types, or categories, of hurricane, based on their greatest wind speed. The Saffir-Simpson Hurricane Wind Scale ranks hurricanes on a scale from 1 to 5, 1 being the weakest, and 5 being the strongest:

- Category 1: 74 to 95 mile-per-hour (129–153 km/h) winds that can damage roof tiles, gutters, power lines and poles, snap large tree branches, and topple some shallow-rooted trees.
- Category 2: 96 to 110 mile-per-hour (154–177 km/h) winds that can damage mobile homes and roofs and blow down trees. These winds can cause power outages.
- Category 3: 111 to 129 mile-per-hour (178–208 km/h) winds that cause more serious damage to buildings, destroy mobile homes, and blow down larger trees.
- Category 4: 130 to 156 mile-per-hour (209–251 km/h) winds can cause so much damage that they can make an area impossible to live in for months.
- Category 5: More than 157 mile-per-hour (252 km/h) winds cause widespread catastrophic damage and damage or destroy almost all buildings and life in their path.

DEADLY DATA

Category 5 hurricane winds blow as fast as some high-speed trains travel.

Wind-whipped waves during a hurricane can dump heavy boats from ports far inland.

CHAPTER 2

WIND POWER

If you were on a boat at sea, you would probably take cover if you saw dark, menacing storm clouds in the distance. Storm clouds often bring heavy rain, but if the conditions are right, they can also grow into ferocious hurricanes.

Storms Form

Air above the ocean is warmed by the sun's rays. The heat also **evaporates** water into **water vapor**. The moist, warm air rises upward because it is lighter than colder air above it. Cold air blows into the gaps left by warm air and is warmed itself. This rise of air is called **convection**. High in the sky, the warm air cools, and the water vapor **condenses** into rain in a cloud. Condensation releases heat energy that helps warm the surrounding air. Rain clouds can change into thunderstorms when temperatures rise. Convection speeds up, and thunderstorm clouds grow tall. At the top of the cloud, it is so cold that water droplets freeze into ice particles. Powerful winds in the cloud bash ice particles together. This process produces **lightning**. Thunder is the sound of air expanding when heated up fast by the incredibly high temperatures of lightning.

The power of a hurricane builds from the sun's warmth heating tropical seas.

Hurricane-force winds whip calm oceans into tall, punishing waves.

Getting Faster

Convection and energy release step up another gear when the ocean water is warm. This heat energy fuels a hurricane. Winds start to spiral faster and faster. A tropical storm has winds of 15.5 miles per hour (25 km/h) or more. When the speeds reach 75 miles per hour (120 km/h), the storm has become a hurricane.

DEADLY DATA

Water at the surface of an ocean needs to be 79° Fahrenheit (26° C) or higher to supply enough energy for hurricane formation. A few degrees can make a big difference to hurricane strength. A category 5 hurricane, Patricia, which blasted Mexico in 2015, was the most powerful ever recorded. It formed over water at 86° Fahrenheit (30° C).

In the Eye

If you could look down on a hurricane from space, you would see a roughly circular mass of clouds with a clear hole in the middle. You might even see the ocean surface through the hole. The hole is a hurricane's eye.

This is a photograph of Hurricane Isabel from 2003 taken by an astronaut in a space station more than 205 miles (330 km) above Earth.

Calm Center

If you were lowered into the eye of a hurricane, it would feel strangely calm. Here, there are no winds and little rain, but the air would be fresh and dry, and the ocean surface would look ruffled. It is here that air sinks downward from high in the sky. There is a clear view upward because there are no clouds in the eye. A hurricane's eye averages 18 to 37 miles (29–60 km) across, so conditions might be still as far as you could see.

Storm Force

The eye is the center of a funnel-shaped column of thunderstorms. Thunderstorms form a wall around the eye, called the eye wall. The eye wall can resemble the banked tiers of a sports stadium. The thunderstorm clouds of the eye wall swirl into the eye like the water spiraling into a plughole when a bathtub is emptying. This wall is where the most powerful winds and driving rain of a hurricane strike.

Spreading Out

Hurricanes' destructive powers do not end with the eye wall. Beyond the eye wall, there are bands of clouds and rain stretching up to hundreds of miles out. These are called rainbands. Rainbands are like fingers of fury that cause disturbance away from the hurricane's eye. For example, the intense rains and push of ocean water by winds can cause flooding of land. When the strong convection and spinning winds move over warm land, they can form tornadoes.

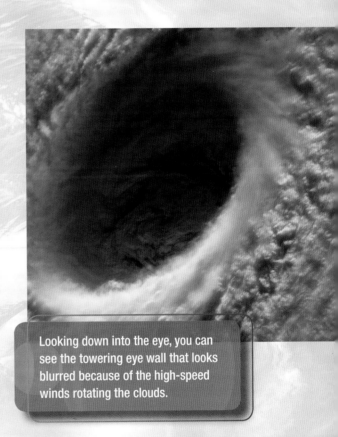

Looking down into the eye, you can see the towering eye wall that looks blurred because of the high-speed winds rotating the clouds.

DEADLY DATA

Hurricanes can causes havoc over large areas. The largest can be more than 600 miles (1,000 km) across. This is the area in which hurricane-force winds blow, but there may be very windy and stormy rainbands beyond this, too.

Hurricanes on the Move

Hurricanes are beasts of the atmosphere that do not stay still. They prowl over oceans and feed on the warmth of the surface waters, growing bigger and bigger.

In 2005, Hurricane Katrina formed off the West Indies and had first **landfall** in Florida. It continued over the Gulf of Mexico before its second landfall on the US Gulf Coast.

Spinning Top

If you have ever played with a spinning top, you have seen how it can move along and change directions. Hurricanes act just the same but over much greater distances. They can travel over thousands of miles of ocean at speeds averaging about 6 miles per hour (9.6 km/h). The track a hurricane takes is not random. Hurricanes cause winds but are also affected by other winds in the atmosphere. For example, there are different **prevailing winds** in different parts of the world's oceans that push hurricanes along, just as they push sailing ships. The track can also be changed when hurricanes pass over mountainous islands, which disrupt the convection processes. Sometimes, a hurricane can slow down to a tropical storm as a result.

Hurricane Death

Hurricanes need two things to form: warm water and regular winds that do not change much in speed or direction as they go up in the sky. A hurricane keeps on track until it reaches land, or makes landfall. Then, it runs out of warm water and will start to die—but not before it has battered coastal land and communities. Winds that change a lot in height can affect the regular spiraling of air in the hurricane and can also cause the hurricane to tilt over. Once the spinning is disrupted and unbalanced, hurricanes lose energy like a spinning plate slowing down.

In 1994, Hurricane John had the longest life of any hurricane in recorded history: 31 days. In this time, it traveled more than 7,000 miles (11,265 km) but amazingly made no landfall, so caused little damage. This is just as well, because its top wind speeds were more than 150 miles per hour (241 km/h).

After landfall and the death of a hurricane, the air may be still. But the damage it causes, such as coastal flooding, is left behind.

CHAPTER 3

HURRICANE ZONES

It may be that you have never heard of a hurricane happening anywhere near where you live. Chances are, that is because you live near a cold ocean, such as the South Atlantic. Hurricanes never start over cold oceans. They get their energy from the warm air that rises above warm water, so they form only over tropical oceans in parts of the world around the **equator**. Once a hurricane gets started, it can travel a long way.

Hurricanes and Cyclones

These wild and dangerous storms are known by different names in different places. When a hurricane happens over the Atlantic and Northeast Pacific Oceans, they are known as hurricanes. When a hurricane occurs in the Northwest Pacific, it is called a typhoon, and in the South Pacific and Indian Ocean, hurricanes are known as cyclones. Even though these events have different names, they are the same kind of storm.

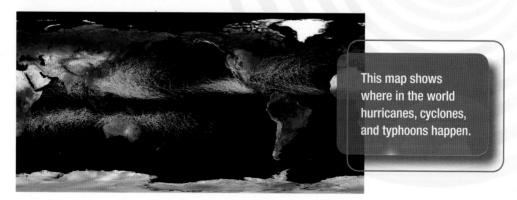

This map shows where in the world hurricanes, cyclones, and typhoons happen.

These dark, dramatic clouds belong to a typhoon that is heading toward the coast of Taiwan.

Spin Cycles

Hurricanes spin in different directions depending on where in the world they occur. This phenomenon happens because Earth is spinning slowly on its **axis** all the time, making one full revolution every 24 hours. As Earth rotates, or turns around, it sweeps the winds blowing above its surface in different directions, curving their movement. In the Northern **Hemisphere**, it pushes the air to the right as it travels northward. In the Southern Hemisphere, it makes winds curve to the left. This explains why hurricane winds starting in the Northern Hemisphere spin around and around in a counterclockwise motion. It also explains why cyclones that originate in the Southern Hemisphere spin in a clockwise motion.

EARTH UNDER ATTACK!

Hurricanes, typhoons, and cyclones may have different names, start in different parts of the world, and even spin in different directions. But otherwise, these deadly storms work in exactly the same way and can cause equal amounts of damage and devastation when they strike a coast.

Hurricane Seasons

Hurricane Sandy was a massive storm in October of the 2012 Atlantic hurricane season.

If you are thinking of traveling to a part of the world that can be affected by hurricanes, typhoons, or cyclones, it is definitely worth picking the time of year that you visit before finalizing plans. Hurricanes do not occur all year round. Hurricanes usually strike during certain times of the year, known as hurricane seasons. Both visitors and locals who live in hurricane zones need to be aware of which months are potentially dangerous.

Save the Date

Hurricanes that form over the North Atlantic occur between June and November each year. Northwest Pacific hurricanes start earlier, in July, and go on until November. In the Northeast Pacific, they start even earlier, in May, and there is still a risk of hurricanes occurring here until November, although the likelihood reduces by then. When hurricane seasons end in one part of the world, they are just beginning in another. In the Southwest Pacific and the South Indian Oceans, hurricanes may appear from October to May. The North Indian Ocean has the longest hurricane season, and it may fall prey to these violent storms at any time from April to December.

Atlantic Peaks

Although Atlantic hurricane season officially begins on June 1, the 8-week period from mid-August to mid-October is the deadliest. This is often the most active and dangerous time for hurricane activity. This is partly because **wind shear** is weakest at this time. Wind shear is when winds suddenly change speed and/or direction over a short distance. When there is less wind shear, hurricane winds are free to spiral upward unhindered. The period of minimum wind shear combines with ocean temperatures that increase with each day of summer sun, creating warmer air and a higher risk of hurricanes.

Catarina was a rare South Atlantic cyclone that formed off the coast of southern Brazil.

EARTH UNDER ATTACK!

Tornadoes, like hurricanes, are fast-spinning windstorms. However, unlike hurricanes, tornadoes start over land, and they can attack at any time of the year, although they are more common through spring and summer when the air is hot enough to create them.

Disaster Report:
2015, Hurricane Patricia

In mid-October 2015, the most violent hurricane to hit Mexico in more than 50 years hit the country. When Hurricane Patricia hit, the peak of the hurricane season was coming to an end, and the Eastern Pacific was hotter than usual. Patricia smashed into Mexico's coastline with wind speeds of more than 200 miles per hour (320 km/h).

The Power of Patricia

Patricia became the 24th named storm of that hurricane season. It was so powerful that its strong winds ripped roofs off houses, destroyed nearly all the trees in its path, and left hillsides bare. It snapped power poles and transmission towers, and it damaged or destroyed more than 10,000 homes. Farmers' livelihoods were in tatters after the hurricane wrecked around 100,000 acres (405 sq km) of farmland where plantains, bananas, and papayas grew. The hurricane dropped heavy rains that caused flooding over a wide area, and as rivers burst their banks, many houses were flooded.

Many tourists had to be **evacuated** from their hotel rooms on the morning of Hurricane Patricia's landfall.

Hurricane Patricia lashed the Mexican coast and caused widespread destruction along the shore.

On the Rampage

Incredibly, this fierce storm killed only six people. Experts monitoring the storm's progress were able to warn people in the towns and villages in Patricia's path that the hurricane was on its way, so they had time to evacuate. Thousands of tourists and local people left the danger zone and made their way out of the area or into the safety of shelters. Airports were closed, and homes and stores were barricaded for protection. The hurricane weakened as it moved inland, especially after colliding with the Sierra Madre mountain range, which absorbed some of its wind power, and it died out.

EARTH UNDER ATTACK!

Two people were killed when Patricia's winds blew a tree onto the tent they were sleeping in at a campsite. Four more people died in a car accident as they drove on a flooded road in the heavy rain.

CHAPTER 4

UNDER ATTACK!

Hurricanes rarely form and track toward land without people knowing about them. People might see and hear warnings on weather or news bulletins on television, internet sites, and radio. However, they can rarely fully imagine the power of a hurricane when it does finally make landfall.

The Buildup

People prepare for the onslaught of a hurricane in the best way they can. For example, they may barricade their windows to keep the glass from breaking. This is not always easy, given that there may already be a tropical storm blowing outside. Soon enough, the first tips of the rainbands of the hurricane are felt. Wind speeds increase, and sea waves become higher and stronger. Coastal trees sway, and the noise of the wind and driving rain gets louder and louder. The buildup continues, and then, the worst part of the hurricane, its eye wall, makes landfall.

Terrifying Winds

Hurricane winds are among the fastest on Earth. They can lift a car, a mobile home, or a billboard into the air and knock it over or even blow it away. The fast-moving air can cave in windows, snap branches or telegraph poles, and blow tiles and other roofing materials off buildings. Dust and soil, leaves, and all kinds of light material are blown around even more easily. All of this debris in the air flies into other objects, causing further damage. Any people on the streets trying to take cover can easily be blown over and risk being injured by flying debris missiles.

The powerful floods caused by Hurricane Sandy in 2012 caved in the windows of stores and other buildings in Brooklyn, New York City, as well as in many other coastal areas.

EARTH UNDER ATTACK!

The impact a hurricane has on coasts depends on how it tracks toward them. A direct landfall is when its track is at right angles to the coast. Then, the intense effects of the storm are concentrated on one piece of land. When the hurricane's track is parallel to and just off the shore, the effects are spread over a larger area of land.

Superstorms

Most people have been caught in rain or even thunderstorms. However, this can give them only the slightest idea of what it is like when vast amounts of water plummet to Earth during a hurricane.

The deluge is so great during a hurricane's rainbands that it is almost impossible to stay dry.

Water Fall

Hurricanes drop huge amounts of water from their rainbands and eye walls. It is not unusual for hurricanes to dump around 3 feet (1 m) of water on the ground surface within a couple of days. The rain is driven hard and fast by the winds. Some water from the storm arrives as hard pellets of ice, too. Hailstones form in thunderstorm clouds as more and more water freezes into layers over the surface of ice particles. Some hailstones can grow to the size of golf balls or grapefruit that are then hurled to Earth by high winds. Hailstones can injure people and damage cars and other objects, especially when they fall in their thousands.

Flooding and Other Problems

All this water on the ground causes short-term **flash floods**. This happens especially on roads and other hard surfaces, because drainage pipes and drains cannot cope with all that water at once. Floods can also persist when the ground becomes **waterlogged**. The rainfall can cause rivers, lakes, canals, and **reservoirs** to spill over their banks, flooding settlements. High rivers running fast can wash away bridges, sections of roads, and cars. Water soaking into hillsides during a hurricane can become very heavy, very quickly. Then, the muddy soil and rocks, along with sections of forest, can slide downhill fast, blocking rivers and burying towns. These landslides are fatal.

Floods during a hurricane pick up, float, and carry away even large and heavy objects, such as motor vehicles, and drop them once the waters recede.

Storm Surge

Hurricane winds and rains are destructive enough. However, the vast majority of deaths from hurricanes happen because of storm surges. A storm surge is when seawater is pushed onto land as the hurricane tracks toward the coastline. This causes deep, fast-moving floods.

How Surges Happen

A hurricane's strong winds push the water ahead of their track. This happens especially on the front right-hand side, because the counterclockwise spinning of the hurricane pushes winds outward most forcibly in this position. Air pressure also causes some of the surge. Air pressure is the push of air downward on Earth's surface. There is so much upward convection in the eye wall that the pressure is low. The low pressure causes a slight bulge of raised seawater in the ocean surface in the hurricane eye. The raised sea level beneath the hurricane contributes even more water to the surge.

Powerful storm surges can wash away supporting soil and concrete under roads, sidewalks, and railroad tracks, so they collapse.

Storm surges can violently throw hundreds of tons of seawater onto land in an instant.

Ocean on Land

The surge of water ahead of a hurricane has little effect in the open, deep ocean. However, when it reaches shallower depths, the water pushed ahead piles up high. At landfall of a big hurricane, a storm surge can be 20 feet (6 m) high and have a width of tens of miles. Surges cause massive coastal flooding. The force of the ocean moving onto land can pick up boats, cars, and homes. These may be carried out to sea once the hurricane passes, and the seawater drains back into the ocean.

EARTH UNDER ATTACK!

Rip currents are dangerous, strong ocean currents away from the shore that can happen when a hurricane approaches. The force of water pushes up an underwater ridge of sand, too. More and more water gets pushed in between coast and ridge, so part of the ridge can collapse. Then surge water on land drains back to the ocean through this gap, creating the rip current. Rip currents can wash even the strongest swimmers far from land.

Disaster Report:
2013, Typhoon Haiyan

Typhoons are not unusual in the Philippines, which gets around 20 each year. Luckily, events such as Haiyan are rare. This massive storm was among the most powerful tropical cyclones to strike land that was ever recorded.

Super Typhoon

Haiyan was a monster! It was more than 500 miles (800 km) in diameter, with an eye 9 miles (14.5 km) wide. When it made landfall in central Philippines, Haiyan, known locally as Yolanda, was rated category 5 on the Saffir-Simpson Scale. The winds in its eye wall peaked at 195 miles per hour (314 km/h), although there were even faster gusts measured at 235 miles per hour (378 km/h). No faster hurricane winds had ever been recorded.

Haiyan's vast storm surge ripped downtown Tacloban buildings and even strong trees to shreds.

Aid workers brought help to Haiyan's victims, including boxes with emergency supplies such as tents and blankets for the affected families.

Super Surge

Typhoon Haiyan's colossal storm surge was deadly. It forced a wall of water 25 feet (7.5 m) high into the city of Tacloban, on the northeast tip of the island of Leyte. Leyte sits fewer than 16 feet (5 m) above sea level. The storm surge washed away people and buildings, leaving areas of muddy ground and debris in its wake. The super surge was so huge and powerful that it washed ashore ships and rolled a rock bigger than a blue whale up a beach.

Hard-Hitting

Haiyan caused massive destruction. In Leyte, around 80 percent of buildings in its path were destroyed. Terrible floods caused by 27 inches (70 cm) of rain also hit Leyte. The central Philippines was worst hit, and altogether, the event affected around 16 million people. The typhoon also killed people in Vietnam and China.

DEADLY DATA

The winds, floods, storm surge, mudslides, and tornado caused by Haiyan killed 7,300 people and destroyed many of the country's coastal farming and fishing communities.

CHAPTER 5

AFTER THE DISASTER

As soon as a hurricane strikes, rescue workers spring into action. In most cases, thousands of emergency service personnel, coast guards, troops, and volunteers reach a disaster area within hours of the hurricane calming or dying out. Every minute counts, and rescuers have to work quickly to treat casualties and save victims from life-threatening situations.

Rescue!

Sometimes rescue workers have to rescue people out of deadly, fast-flowing floodwater. Pilots hold their helicopters rock-steady as they hover above flooded or remote land while their crew lowers rescue baskets to lift survivors to safety. Emergency workers may string ropes across rivers to catch people who are caught up in speeding waters, or travel by boat through flooded city streets to rescue people trapped on the roofs or upper floors of their homes. Not everyone can swim to safety, and floodwaters often hide dangerous animals such as poisonous snakes, so it is not safe to be in them. Firefighters help rescue survivors and put out fires caused by downed power lines. In some places, helicopters airlift people to safety, especially from remote regions where floods have cut off roads.

First Responders

Doctors and nurses arrive to give emergency medical care to casualties at the scene of the disaster. They patch up wounds and give immediate assistance to make victims stable enough to travel, so they can be transported to a nearby hospital. Sometimes medics set up field hospitals (temporary hospitals) near a disaster so victims do not have too far to travel and can be treated for serious injuries as soon as possible.

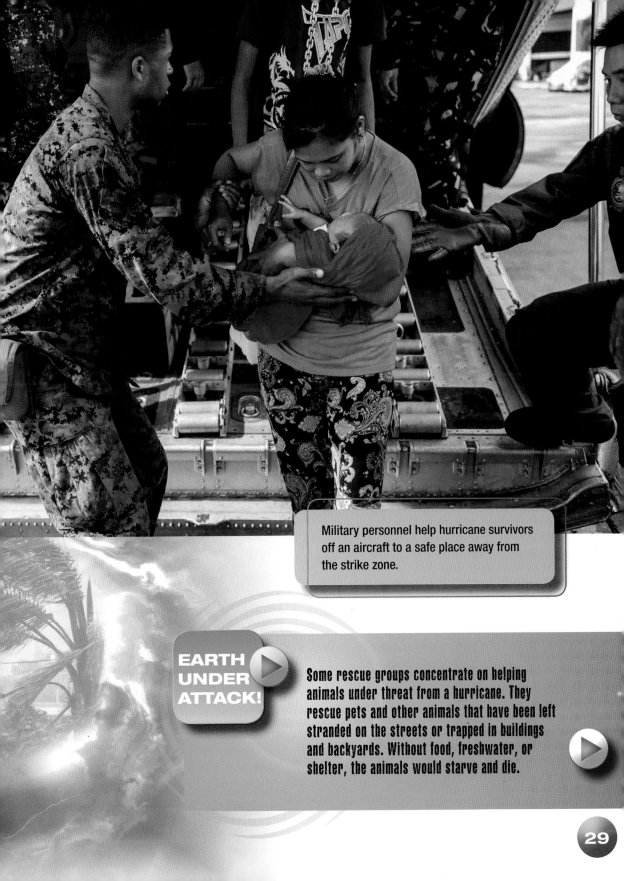

Military personnel help hurricane survivors off an aircraft to a safe place away from the strike zone.

EARTH UNDER ATTACK!

Some rescue groups concentrate on helping animals under threat from a hurricane. They rescue pets and other animals that have been left stranded on the streets or trapped in buildings and backyards. Without food, freshwater, or shelter, the animals would starve and die.

Saving Survivors

The work does not stop after victims have been rescued from immediate danger and the floodwaters start to subside. The period of calm after a hurricane can be just as deadly as the storm itself. Emergency workers, volunteers, and helpers from **aid organizations** play a vital role in keeping survivors safe.

Volunteers help the military and other agencies unload and distribute aid. This may need to continue for months after an event before life gets back to normal.

Safe Shelter

People who have escaped or have been evacuated from their homes need somewhere safe to stay. Governments and aid organizations set up temporary shelters or arrange for people to stay nearby in gymnasiums and halls. They bring the blankets, food, and medical supplies that survivors need. They bring games for children to play. They also bring supplies of clean drinking water, because people cannot drink or use dirty floodwater or water from damaged pipes. **Contaminated** water is a real threat since it can carry dangerous diseases.

Dealing with Dangers

After a hurricane, streets and buildings can be flooded with a whirlpool of sludge that consists of human waste and harmful chemicals. There are other problems to sort out, too. Emergency workers travel around the area fixing fallen power lines that could **electrocute** people. They also cut down trees that are badly damaged and could fall and injure passersby. They check buildings for damage, and they may board up any that are too dangerous to reenter.

EARTH UNDER ATTACK!

Natural disasters in less-developed countries can cause longer-term problems. People there may not have insurance to help them pay to rebuild their homes and restart their businesses. Governments may not have the resources to help their people. In countries like this, the work of aid organizations, such as the Red Cross or Care International, is especially important. These organizations often ship food, tents, blankets, and medical supplies to countries where people need help.

Clean, bottled drinking water is a vital aid to keep people from becoming sick after a hurricane, when storm surge flooding ruins water supplies.

Counting Losses

It takes a lot of time and money for things to return to normal after a major hurricane disaster. Whole towns and cities may need to be reconstructed, and people who have lost everything in the storm need help rebuilding their lives.

Reconstruction

People must work to clear roads of obstructions and debris, such as fallen trees, battered boats, or parts of buildings washed inland by floods. After removing the rubble, they start to repair broken bridges and rebuild homes, schools, hospitals, churches, and other public buildings. In some regions of the world, where hurricanes rip apart tin houses and turn the fragments of flying metal into deadly missiles, people try to build new houses from different, safer materials.

The high winds of a cyclone in New Zealand have damaged this corn crop.

Lost Livelihoods

Governments and aid organizations help people return to work. When hurricanes ruin crops and farmland, organizations may provide tools, farm animals, and seeds or young plants, so that people can start growing food for themselves again.

Storm surges wreck ships and harbors, killing fish and robbing fishermen and women of the chance to make a living. Providing these people with new boats and rebuilding harbors where they work breathes new life into damaged coastal communities.

Comfort and Recovery

People may also need help recovering from the trauma of a hurricane. Some organizations set up child-friendly spaces to provide children who are unable to go to school with spaces to play. They also offer the support of trained staff and counselors, who help adults deal with the emotional effects of the hurricane.

Hurricane Irene's storm surge flooded fish from fish farm tanks. They were left aground and dead when the floodwaters drained away.

EARTH UNDER ATTACK!

Many people lose everything in a hurricane disaster. When they get off the rescue bus and walk into a shelter, they may have only the clothes on their backs. Everything else—their homes, businesses, and all their possessions—has been destroyed.

Disaster Report:
2005, Hurricane Katrina

When Hurricane Katrina hit New Orleans in the early hours of August 29, 2005, it was a vicious category 5 storm. Katrina killed 1,850 people, caused destruction up to 150 miles (240 km) inland, and left more than 500,000 homeless. It was the deadliest hurricane to hit the United States in 75 years.

Raging Winds

Hurricane Katrina's powerful winds raged at 125 miles per hour (200 km/h). They snapped trees, blasted through buildings, and broke power lines that started fires. The hurricane also brought torrential rains and severe flooding. Floodwaters broke through the banks of earth, called **levees**, that had been built around the city (which lies below sea level), in the hope of preventing flooding. The floodwater smashed through the levees and flooded about 80 percent of the city. In some places, the water was 20 feet (6 m) deep and washed poisonous snakes, dirt, rocks, and debris into streets and buildings.

Helicopter rescue crews survey the catastrophic flood damage to New Orleans residential areas after Katrina.

In just a few days, the New Orleans Superdome was transformed from a sports arena to an emergency shelter for thousands of people left homeless by the floods.

Evacuation Errors

There had been evacuation warnings, and 2 million people did escape before the hurricane hit, but many chose to stay in New Orleans or could not get away in time. Many people were killed by the flooding, while others smashed holes in attic roofs to escape the waters and waited to be rescued by helicopter or boat. Around 30,000 survivors were taken to the city's Superdome, but no food or water arrived. People suffered hot and terrible conditions here for up to 4 or 5 days before being taken elsewhere.

Rebuilding Lives

The damage caused by Hurricane Katrina made it the most expensive natural disaster ever to strike the United States. The cost of evacuating residents, finding them shelter and food, pumping out floodwater, and clearing debris took a lot of time and money before the government could start to think about rebuilding the city.

DEADLY DATA

The total cost of the damage caused by Hurricane Katrina was more than $100 billion.

CHAPTER 6

LIVING IN A HURRICANE ZONE

Given how dangerous hurricanes can be, you might think it surprising that anyone would want to live in a hurricane zone. However, in most cases, scientists who study hurricanes can use early warning systems that allow plenty of time for people to evacuate safely. People can also build safer homes and emergency shelters to help them stay safe.

Hurricane Shelters

If you live in an area where there is even a chance of flooding, you should evacuate as soon as possible. If flooding is unlikely, people should go into a storm shelter. In places where hurricanes are frequent, there are public storm shelters where many people can go. Some families may buy or build their own shelters near their homes. Stand-alone hurricane shelters are usually constructed from steel panels that are welded together into a box shape, or they are made from concrete. They have a strong steel door, and they are bolted to a concrete base that can withstand high winds and flying debris. Other people have a safe room inside their house. This is a room, usually a basement, that is specially strengthened, or reinforced, for protection.

Safe Houses

People can also take measures to make existing buildings safer. They can attach strong storm panels or shutters to windows that protect the glass during a storm. They can cut off dead branches and cut down old trees that could easily be toppled by hurricane winds. People also attach metal straps or clips to connect the roof to exterior walls. To prevent floods, governments build strong storm surge drains that let more water soak away, and they build stronger bridges to cope with violent wind and rain.

Hurricane evacuation route signs were in place in New Orleans long before Katrina struck. The dark lines on the signs show the height that Katrina's floodwaters reached on this street.

EARTH UNDER ATTACK! ▶ On some coasts, people have built seawalls to protect seaside towns from storm surges. In 1900, the hurricane that hit Galveston, Texas, on the coast of the Gulf of Mexico killed 6,000 people. Some of its residents built a massive seawall to turn back storm-generated waves. It has protected Galveston ever since and has even survived, though not unscathed, powerful category 4 Hurricane Ike in 2009.

Hurricane Hunters

Most pilots would be careful to steer their aircraft away from a raging hurricane. However, when hurricane hunters hear of a hurricane brewing at sea, they set off on daring missions into the eye of the storm. Their goal is to collect information about the storm, so that they can understand hurricanes better and help forecasters make better predictions about the size, strength, speed, track, and likely landfall of any future hurricanes.

Flying Laboratories

Expert pilots guide the aircraft through the extreme wind and rain of the hurricane's rainbands and eye wall. They do this aboard a flying laboratory, so that they can give scientists access to the storm up close. Scientists use a variety of equipment to collect data. For example, **radar** systems send out radio waves through the storm and record reflections of the signals. Radar scans can calculate where rain is falling and the structure of hurricane storm clouds. Other devices on board can measure ocean surface conditions, which are useful in predicting a storm surge.

Hurricane Hunters head off toward an approaching tropical storm that could grow into a hurricane. They fly aboard a specialist aircraft fitted with wind-measuring radar.

A **meteorologist** working at Hickam Air Force Base in Hawaii views data sent from a Hurricane Hunter aircraft to help track and monitor the growth of a hurricane.

Mini Weather Stations

Scientists release devices called dropsondes into the storm, and these act like mini weather stations. Dropsondes are cylinders packed with **sensors** that automatically collect data on the temperature, wind speed, and moisture in the air. The dropsondes relay these data back to computers on board the aircraft as they fall or are blown through the storm. Dropsondes have **GPS** trackers built in, similar to GPS systems in cars, so that scientists know exactly where the data is coming from.

EARTH UNDER ATTACK!

Hurricane Hunters are under great threat from the storm, so they increasingly use flying robots, or drones, to collect data. Using handsets, pilots on the ground control the drones. Drones do not become tired like pilots, and there is no loss of life if they crash.

Early Warning Systems

Once a storm has formed, Hurricane Hunters get up close with the storm and track it toward coastlines. They get highly detailed data, but this is not always enough to help with early warnings of hurricane formation. In order to have a fuller picture of where and why hurricanes form and their exact routes, it helps to have a more distant view from space!

Above Earth

High above Earth's atmosphere on the fringes of space, there are **satellites** moving around our planet. Some of these machines hold a fixed position that GPS trackers compare their position to. Others help relay computer files, phone messages, and other data from one side of the planet to another. Weather satellites help study hurricanes. Cameras on the satellites take regular pictures of oceans to spot new storms and to record how they grow. Special heat-sensitive cameras detect ocean surface temperatures, while other sensors measure rainfall patterns and hurricane eye shapes through the clouds.

Satellites **orbit** high above Earth carrying equipment that can help us view and understand hurricanes at the planet's surface.

Forecasting

Hurricane Hunters and weather satellites produce millions of pieces of different data. Powerful computers are programmed by meteorologists to handle the data. The programs generate 3D animations of storms that show their shape, direction, and speed of movement. The images are updated as new data is received. Meteorologists produce hurricane forecasts of strength, track, and storm surge using the data and images. News channels broadcast forecasts, and governments and emergency services use them to prepare for the approaching storm. However, no forecast can be exact because so many factors affect hurricanes. For example, unexpected warm currents of water in oceans can produce a stronger hurricane than forecast.

Weather forecasters tell people what weather and extreme events to expect. This news may come via regular television news bulletins, radio shows, or web pages.

DEADLY DATA

Meteorologists are much less certain where a hurricane will strike 120 hours (5 days) in advance than 24 hours in advance. This is because hurricanes can shift track so much at sea. A landfall forecasted 5 days ahead could be off by as much as 350 miles (563 km). This uncertainty drops to 100 miles (161 km) 24 hours before landfall.

What to Do in a Hurricane

When a hurricane strikes, it is vital that everyone is well informed and ready for action. If people know what to do, they are more likely to stay calm, which increases their chances of reaching a safe place.

Stay Alert!

When it comes to surviving a hurricane, the first rule is to stay informed. During hurricane season, people should watch the news, listen to the radio, and check online forecasts to find out more information about the situation in their area. People sometimes have several days to prepare for a hurricane, or they may need to move more quickly. As soon as there is an actual hurricane alert, they should decide whether to stay or go. Local authorities should advise whether people have time to evacuate the area or go to a shelter.

A family in Mississippi prepares its supplies and checks an evacuation route map before the start of hurricane season.

An evacuation order caused thousands of people to hit the highway out of New Orleans before Hurricane Katrina made landfall in Louisiana in 2005.

Planning Ahead

Every family, school, office, and other building in a hurricane zone should have an evacuation plan and emergency kits. An evacuation plan tells people where the nearest shelter is and what to bring with them. People should also know which routes to travel and who to ask for a ride if they do not have a car. An emergency kit should contain essential items that help people while they are in a shelter or if they have to evacuate. It might include nonperishable food, clothes, bedding, a first-aid kit, medicines, flashlight and batteries, a cell phone, important papers, such as identity documents and driver's licenses, and a supply of drinking water.

EARTH UNDER ATTACK!

Understanding hurricanes can keep people alive. The eye of the hurricane is the calmest part of the storm, and some people get lured out of their home or shelter because they think the storm has passed. Then, they get caught in the violent winds from the opposite side of the eye wall.

Future Hurricanes

Hurricanes are incredible forces of nature that will continue into the future. They will happen wherever the dangerous combination of warm ocean surfaces and stable wind patterns exists. However, their frequency and strength could change as a result of **global warming**.

Changing Atmosphere

Most scientists agree that Earth's atmosphere is getting warmer. This is happening because human activities, such as burning fuels in power plants, are creating more gases, such as carbon dioxide, which stick around in the atmosphere. The gases store heat from the sun, so the planet very gradually becomes warmer. This global warming is changing weather patterns around the world. For example, it is making formerly warm areas cooler. Meteorologists are predicting stronger, more damaging hurricanes and tornadoes as a result of warming oceans. Factors such as rising sea levels due to melting polar ice and warmer water that takes up more space in oceans could also result in more catastrophic storm surges.

Floodwaters rise in Texas because of a surge long before Hurricane Ike makes landfall. With higher sea levels, surges will cause more widespread flooding.

Better Prediction

Scientists are already developing tools to better understand hurricanes and make more accurate forecasts of these killer storms. In 2016, US space scientists launched a group of small satellites called the Cyclone Global Navigation Satellite System into orbit. These satellites are fitted with sensors that can look inside hurricanes to collect frequent and highly accurate data, such as ocean surface wind speeds, in the eye and eye wall of hurricanes. This information should help improve forecasts of hurricane intensity.

People can live alongside hurricanes so long as they are prepared and vigilant, and where possible, can keep out of their way.

EARTH UNDER ATTACK!

Scientists have found a link between one of the driest places on Earth, the Sahara, and hurricanes. Dust storms blow west from the Sahara over the Atlantic. This dust reflects the sun's heat, making the ocean slightly cooler. In the future, meteorologists believe that global warming will change wind patterns as more air warms up. This will reduce winds and dust storms from Africa. Then, the Atlantic will warm, and more hurricanes could form.

45

GLOSSARY

aid organizations groups that raise money and provide help for people in need

atmosphere blanket of gases that surround Earth

axis an imaginary line drawn through the North Pole and the South Pole of Earth

condenses changes from a gas to a liquid

contaminated dirty and unsafe to use

convection when the warmer parts in a gas or liquid move up and the colder parts move down

debris fragments of trees, building rubble, or vehicles broken up by, for example, hurricane winds

electrocute to injure or kill with electricity

equator imaginary line around the center of Earth dividing it into two halves, the Northern and Southern Hemispheres

evacuated moved to somewhere safe to escape danger

evaporates turns from a liquid into a gas

flash floods sudden, dramatic floods that usually happen because of very heavy rainfall

floods when large amounts of water cover land that is usually dry

global warming gradual rise in Earth's average temperature

GPS an acronym for Global Positioning System: a navigation system that uses satellites to pinpoint locations

hemisphere half of the Earth

landfall arriving on land

landslides when rock, mud, and debris break off and slide down a slope

levees raised walls that prevent flooding of a river or other body of water

lightning flash of light in the sky caused by electricity moving between clouds or between a cloud and the Earth's surface

meteorologist a scientist who studies Earth's atmosphere and weather

orbit to move in space on a curved path around a planet or star

prevailing winds winds that blow mainly from one direction.

radar system using radio waves to locate objects at a distance

reservoirs man-made lakes of water used as a water supply

satellites man-made objects in orbit above Earth that can take images of Earth's atmosphere

sensors machines that sense or measure different things, such as temperature or wind speed

tornadoes violent windstorms consisting of a tall column of air that spins around

water vapor water in the form of a gas

waterlogged full of water

wind shear sudden change in wind speed and/or direction

FOR MORE INFORMATION

BOOKS

Bowman, Chris. *Survive a Hurricane* (Survival Zone). Hopkins, MN: Bellwether Media, 2016.

Elkins, Elizabeth. *Investigating Hurricanes* (Investigating Natural Disasters). North Mankato, MN: Capstone, 2017.

Kostigan, Thomas M. *Extreme Weather: Surviving Tornadoes, Sandstorms, Hailstorms, Blizzards, Hurricanes, and More!* (National Geographic Kids). Washington, DC: National Geographic, 2014.

Philbrick, Rodman. *Zane and the Hurricane: A Story of Katrina*. New York, NY: The Blue Sky Press, 2015.

Winchester, Simon. *When the Sky Breaks: Hurricanes, Tornadoes, and the Worst Weather in the World* (Smithsonian). New York, NY: Viking, 2017.

WEBSITES

Learn more about tsunamis at:
www.ngkids.co.uk/science-and-nature/tsunamis

Discover how to prepare for a tsunami at:
www.ready.gov/tsunamis

Check out an interactive guide to tsunamis at:
www.whoi.edu/home/interactive/tsunami/indexEnglish.html

Find more information about tsunamis at:
www.dkfindout.com/uk/earth/earthquakes/tsunami/

Publisher's note to educators and parents: Our editors have carefully reviewed these websites to ensure that they are suitable for students. Many websites change frequently, however, and we cannot guarantee that a site's future contents will continue to meet our high standards of quality and educational value. Be advised that students should be closely supervised whenever they access the Internet.

INDEX